T0199167

To the Graduate:
A Recipe for Success

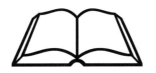

By Dr. Patula Mandrozos and Fotini Mamos

WestBow Press books may be ordered through booksellers or by contacting:

WestBow Press
A Division of Thomas Nelson & Zondervan
1663 Liberty Drive
Bloomington, IN 47403
www.westbowpress.com
1 (866) 928-1240

ISBN: 978-1-9736-5189-5 (sc)
ISBN: 978-1-9736-5190-1 (e)

Library of Congress Control Number: 2019900870

Print information available on the last page.

WestBow Press rev. date: 02/25/2019

WestBow
PRESS®
A DIVISION OF THOMAS NELSON
& ZONDERVAN

Dear Graduate,
As you embark on your journey for education, we hope that these words will inspire and motivate you to reach higher and pursue your goals with courage and perseverance.

When embarking on a project in life, it is always best to have a plan and as with all plans, a recipe is required. As with all recipes, this recipe too has a sequence of steps that must be followed.

First of all, in order to succeed, you must first find where your passion lies. This should not be something that you like well enough, but something that you love. Find the ONE thing that ignites a fire in your soul, and then, PURSUE IT!

Make big choices and take some risks. You will never know what lies around the corner if you don't take a peek.

So follow your HEART and TRUST yourself.

Once you have discovered your passion, the second step is to put down your cell phone. Become engaged with the world. Don't bury yourself in texts.

Open your eyes and look at
the beauty that is our world.

When you are talking you cannot listen, and you must listen to learn. Listen to your professors and mentors. You may not always agree, but learn to listen and form opinions that will become who you are.

Surround yourself with
people and friends who
will inspire and challenge
you.

Remember, you are
going to college to learn.
If you don't know or
don't understand
something, have the
courage to admit it and
then,
LEARN!

The third ingredient in this recipe for success is hard work. There is no substitute for your own toil for what you really want. Don't be afraid to go the extra mile. Do the things that no one will do. If you work harder and longer, people will notice.

The world DOES NOT OWE YOU ANYTHING and you should NEVER consider yourself a VICTIM!

You have the ability and
intelligence to empower
yourself.
Cultivate your mind so
that you may rightfully
earn a place of honor
and respect.

It won't be easy, and many times you will be scared and afraid, but when this happens, hold someones hand so that they can help you.

And when you are brave, show that same compassion and take someone with you.

The last part of this secret recipe is:

BELIEVE
IN
YOURSELF,

But most of all,

BELIEVE
IN
GOD

HE got you here and HE knows where you need to go.

So, stay true to your roots. Return the love that your family, friends, and religion have bestowed upon you.

And perhaps in the end, you can be like Odysseus in his quest to find Ithaca.

ΜΟΛΩΝ ΛΑΒΕ

-Thankful for the journey and a life well lived!

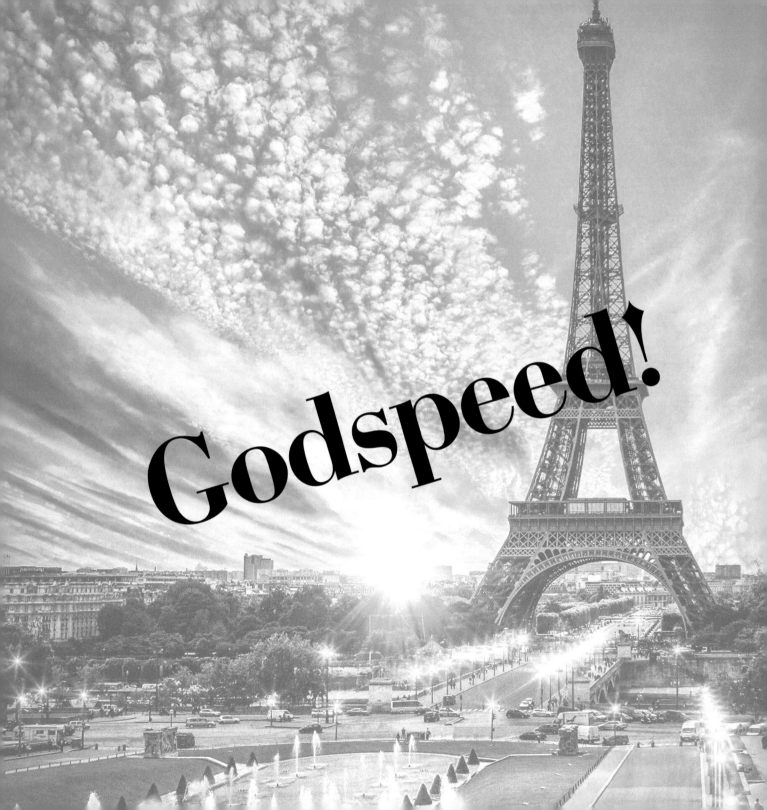

Author Biography

 **Dr. Mandrozos** graduated from NYU undergraduate and Stoney Brook School of Dental Medicine. She has been practicing dentistry for 30 years and has held multiple positions, including president of the AGD, Queens Chapter. As a fellow of the AGD, Dr. Mandrozos has taught dentistry to the residents of Flushing Hospital Medical Center in the capacity of an attending at the clinic. Fotini Mamos graduated from Saint Francis Preparatory School with top honors. She was on the National Honors Society and a member of the National Society of High School Scholars. This speech was given by Fotini Mamos at the commencement ceremony for the graduating class of Saint Francis Prep in 2016. Presently, Fotini is studying at Queens College, where she is pursuing a double major in Nutrition and Fashion Designing.

Printed in the United States
By Bookmasters